W9-AET-960

CHECKERBOARD BIOGRAPHY LIBRARY

U.S. PRESIDENTS

The United States Presidents

JAMES K. POLK

ABDO Publishing Company

BreAnn Rumsch

visit us at
www.abdopublishing.com

Published by ABDO Publishing Company, 8000 West 78th Street, Edina, Minnesota 55439.
Copyright © 2009 by Abdo Consulting Group, Inc. International copyrights reserved in all
countries. No part of this book may be reproduced in any form without written permission from the
publisher. The Checkerboard Library™ is a trademark and logo of ABDO Publishing Company.

Printed in the United States.

Cover Photo: Getty Images
Interior Photos: Alamy pp. 9, 29; Corbis pp. 5, 25; Getty Images pp. 11, 19, 23; iStockphoto p. 32;
     Library of Congress pp. 13, 16, 17, 21; National Archives p. 27; North Wind pp. 22, 26;
     Picture History p. 14; Public Domain p. 8

Editor: Heidi M.D. Elston
Art Direction & Cover Design: Neil Klinepier
Interior Design: Neil Klinepier

Library of Congress Cataloging-in-Publication Data
Rumsch, BreAnn, 1981-
 James K. Polk / BreAnn Rumsch.
     p. cm. -- (United States presidents)
 Includes index.
 ISBN 978-1-60453-470-2
 1. Polk, James K. (James Knox), 1795-1849--Juvenile literature. 2. Presidents--United States--
Biography--Juvenile literature. I. Title.

 E417.R86 2009
 973.6'1--dc22
 [B]
                              2008042606

CONTENTS

JAMES K. POLK

James K. Polk was the eleventh president of the United States. As president, he took steps to establish an independent **treasury**. Polk also established the border between the Oregon country and Canada. And, he led the United States in a war against Mexico.

Polk grew up on a farm in Tennessee. He did not attend school until he was 17. Yet, he worked hard and was a good student. Three years later, he entered the University of North Carolina in Chapel Hill. Soon after graduation, Polk became a successful lawyer.

Polk later served in the Tennessee legislature and the U.S. House of Representatives. Then, he became governor of Tennessee. In 1844, he was nominated for president. His nomination surprised many people. This made Polk the first dark horse president.

President Polk worked hard to lead America. He took responsibility for shaping the nation. During his presidency, he helped the country gain more than 500,000 square miles (1.3 million sq km) of land. By the end of Polk's term, the United States stretched from coast to coast.

James K Polk

TIMELINE

1795 - On November 2, James Knox Polk was born in Mecklenburg County, North Carolina.

1818 - Polk graduated at the top of his class from the University of North Carolina in Chapel Hill.

1819 - Polk became a clerk in the Tennessee state senate.

1823 - Polk won election to the Tennessee House of Representatives.

1824 - On January 1, Polk married Sarah Childress.

1825 - Polk won election to the U.S. House of Representatives.

1835 - Polk became Speaker of the House.

1839 - Polk became governor of Tennessee.

1844 - At the Democratic National Convention, Polk became the first dark horse candidate to run for president.

1845 - On March 4, Polk became the eleventh U.S. president.

1846 - Congress passed the Walker Tariff Act and the Independent Treasury Act; the United States and England signed the Oregon Treaty, settling the boundary question; on May 13, Congress declared war on Mexico.

1848 - On February 2, the United States and Mexico signed the Treaty of Guadalupe Hidalgo, which ended the Mexican War; the United States acquired the Mexican Cession.

1849 - On March 3, Congress established the Department of the Interior; on June 15, James K. Polk died at his home in Nashville, Tennessee.

DID YOU KNOW?

James K. Polk kept a diary throughout his life. In it, he often referred to himself as "the President" during his term in office.

During Polk's presidency, the U.S. Naval Academy was founded on October 10, 1845. Polk's secretary of the navy, George Bancroft, established it in Annapolis, Maryland.

On August 10, 1846, Polk signed an act establishing the Smithsonian Institution in Washington, D.C. Today, the institution is the world's largest museum complex and research facility. It is home to 19 museums and 9 research centers.

Gold was discovered in California on January 28, 1848. In a speech delivered on December 5, Polk confirmed the discovery. At that time, the California gold rush began.

PRESIDENT OF THE
POTUS
UNITED STATES

TENNESSEE YOUTH

James Knox Polk was born on November 2, 1795, in Mecklenburg County, North Carolina. His parents, Samuel and Jane Polk, were farmers. James was the oldest of their ten children.

When James was 11, his family moved to Columbia, Tennessee.

The only surviving Polk family home stands in Columbia, Tennessee. James lived in the house from 1818 to 1824.

James was small for his age. He was often sick, so he could not help on the farm. James could not go to school either. Instead, he was **tutored** at home.

FAST FACTS

BORN - November 2, 1795

WIFE - Sarah Childress (1803–1891)

CHILDREN - None

POLITICAL PARTY - Democrat

AGE AT INAUGURATION - 49

YEARS SERVED - 1845–1849

VICE PRESIDENT - George M. Dallas

DIED - June 15, 1849, age 53

The University of North Carolina

When James was 16, he had an operation. A well-known doctor named Ephraim McDowell performed the surgery. Doctor McDowell removed **gallstones** from James's **gallbladder**. James felt much better after the operation. In time, he became stronger and healthier.

In July 1813, James began attending a nearby school. The next year, he entered the Murfreesboro Academy in Tennessee. James loved learning and studied hard.

James took an entrance examination for college when he was 20. He passed the test and entered the University of North Carolina. James was admitted to the second-year class. He quickly became one of the university's best students. James was also skilled in **debate**. In 1818, he graduated at the top of his class.

LAW AND MARRIAGE

After graduation, Polk decided to become a lawyer. He moved to Nashville, Tennessee. There, he began working for Felix Grundy. Grundy had been a Kentucky **Supreme Court** judge and a U.S. congressman. Polk learned much about law from Grundy's experience.

Grundy also helped Polk become a clerk in the Tennessee state senate in 1819. Polk worked hard as a clerk. Meanwhile, he kept studying to be a lawyer. In 1820, Polk passed his lawyer's examination. He then returned to Columbia and opened his own law firm.

About this same time, Polk met Sarah Childress. She was the daughter of a successful businessman. Sarah was outgoing and well educated. Polk enjoyed Sarah's company and eventually asked her to marry him. The couple married on January 1, 1824. They had a large country wedding. The Polks had no children.

Mr. and Mrs. Polk were devoted to one another throughout their lives.

REPRESENTATIVE POLK

Meanwhile, Polk decided to run for the Tennessee House of Representatives. He won the election in 1823. As a Tennessee representative, Polk worked to lower taxes and improve state schools. Polk also supported General Andrew Jackson for president in 1824. But Jackson lost the election.

In 1825, Polk decided to run for the U.S. House of Representatives. He won the election! Soon, he left Tennessee for Washington, D.C.

Polk was one of the youngest members serving in the House. He was reelected to the House six times. He served from 1825 to 1839. Polk was an honest, hardworking congressman.

In 1828, Polk once again helped Jackson campaign for president. This time, Jackson won. He took office the following year.

In Congress, Polk fully supported President Jackson's policies. Like Jackson, Polk opposed spending federal money on state improvement projects. He also supported Jackson's high **tariff** bills.

Andrew Jackson

In his 14 years of service, Polk was absent from Congress only once.

At this time, the Bank of the United States was the national bank. It was set to expire in 1836. So in 1832, Congress approved a bill to renew it. However, President Jackson opposed the bank and **vetoed** the bill.

Congressman Polk also opposed the bank. In 1833, he became chairman of the House Committee on Ways and Means. As chairman, Polk supported removing federal deposits from the bank. This caused the bank to struggle. As a result, it expired as planned.

In 1835, Polk became **Speaker of the House**. As Speaker, Polk worked to keep order in the House. This was especially important during **debates** on slavery.

Polk believed Congress had no authority to act on slavery. He thought each state should decide for themselves if they would allow slavery. Polk's opinion upset many antislavery representatives. Still, Polk was a fair Speaker. He believed everyone had a right to share his or her opinion.

Polk served as Speaker of the House until 1839. Then, Jackson persuaded him to run for governor of Tennessee. Polk won the election. He served as governor from 1839 to 1841. Polk ran for governor two more times, but he was not reelected.

DARK HORSE ELECTION

After facing defeat in Tennessee, Polk wanted to return to national politics. He hoped the **Democrats** would nominate him for vice president.

In 1844, the **Democratic National Convention** was held in Baltimore, Maryland. The party could not agree on a candidate for president.

The Democrats voted seven times. But no candidate received enough votes to be nominated. Then, they decided to compromise. They added Polk as a candidate for president.

On the eighth vote, Polk was third in line to win the nomination. Former president Martin Van Buren and Senator

Martin Van Buren was president from 1837 to 1841.

16

Lewis Cass of Michigan were ahead of him. But on the ninth vote, every representative voted for Polk!

Finally, the party was united behind one candidate. Polk's nomination had come as a surprise. So, he became known as the dark horse candidate. Polk was the first dark horse candidate to run in a U.S. presidential election. George M. Dallas of Pennsylvania became his **running mate**.

Before 1844, Democratic delegates had never needed to vote multiple times to name a nominee.

The **Whig** Party nominated Henry Clay for president. He would be a tough opponent for Polk to beat. Clay had served in the U.S. House of Representatives and the U.S. Senate. He had also been **secretary of state** under President John Quincy Adams. Clay's **running mate** was New Jersey senator Theodore Frelinghuysen.

At the time, much conflict centered on expanding the United States. Americans discussed if Texas should be a state. They also argued whether or not it should have slavery. In addition, they wondered where the Oregon country's northern border should be.

These issues became important during the campaign. Clay was against **annexing** Texas. But Polk supported it. Polk also wanted to claim the Oregon country north to the fifty-fourth **parallel**. The fifty-fourth parallel would mark the boundary between the United States and Canada.

Polk made sure Americans heard his ideas. The **Democratic** Party's campaign **slogan** became "Fifty-four Forty or Fight!" Many people agreed with Polk. Still, the Whigs tried to beat Polk. They said he was a compromise candidate. They also pointed out that he was not well known. Their slogan became "Who is James K. Polk?" Yet Polk won the election!

Henry Clay

PRESIDENT POLK

Polk was **inaugurated** on March 4, 1845. At the time, he was just 49 years old. This made him younger than any previous president.

As president, Polk had four goals. He wanted to lower **tariffs** and make a new U.S. **treasury**. He also wanted to establish a border between the Oregon country and Canada. And, he hoped to claim California for the United States.

Polk's **secretary of the treasury**, Robert J. Walker, **drafted** a new tariff. In 1846, Congress passed the Walker Tariff Act. The act lowered tariffs on some imported goods. This was the first tariff drafted by the executive branch.

Less than a week later, Congress passed the Independent Treasury Act. This act helped form the nation's financial system. And, the independent treasury would keep federal money separate from private and state banks. Polk believed this would help prevent financial problems in the future.

**SUPREME
COURT
APPOINTMENTS**

LEVI WOODBURY - 1845
ROBERT C. GRIER - 1846

Polk was inaugurated outside the U.S. Capitol.
The ceremony took place in the rain.

THE OREGON TREATY

Back in 1818, England and the United States had signed a treaty. In it, both countries agreed to share the Oregon country. This area of land was west of the Rocky Mountains. It included land between present-day Alaska and California.

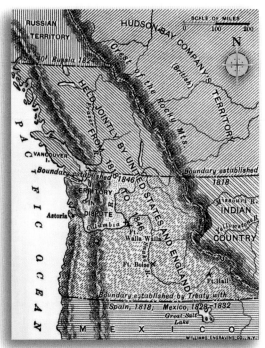

The Oregon country was occupied jointly by the United States and England until 1846.

Now, many congressmen wanted to end the agreement. They thought the United States should claim its share of the land. They wanted the boundary set north of the fifty-fourth **parallel**.

However, President Polk knew that neither nation could claim the entire territory. So in 1846, he instructed **Secretary of State** James Buchanan to offer England a compromise. Buchanan proposed a new boundary set farther south at the forty-ninth parallel. However, England refused the offer.

James Buchanan

Polk did not want to fight England over the land. Yet he stood firm. Polk then told Buchanan to claim the whole area for the United States. England decided Polk's first offer was better.

That year, the two countries signed the Oregon Treaty. It set the border at the forty-ninth **parallel**. The U.S. land included present-day Oregon, Washington, and Idaho. It also included parts of Montana and Wyoming. England gained full control of Vancouver Island.

President Polk had settled the border question peacefully. Unfortunately, another border disagreement would lead to war.

WAR WITH MEXICO

On December 29, 1845, Texas had become part of the United States. But, Mexico still wanted to control Texas. In addition, the two nations disagreed about which river created the new state's southern border. Mexico believed the boundary was the Nueces River. The United States said the Rio Grande was the boundary.

Mexican officials refused to meet with Congressman John Slidell. Polk had sent Slidell to buy California and settle the Texas border disagreement.

In January 1846, Polk sent U.S. troops to Texas. They occupied the area in question. Mexico considered this an invasion. So on April 25, Mexican soldiers crossed the Rio Grande. They attacked the American troops there. About 16 American soldiers were injured or killed.

On May 11, President Polk asked Congress to declare war. He said Mexico had "invaded our territory and shed American blood on American soil." Two days later, Congress declared war on Mexico.

PRESIDENT POLK'S CABINET

MARCH 4, 1845–
MARCH 4, 1849

- **STATE –** James Buchanan
- **TREASURY –** Robert J. Walker
- **WAR –** William Learned Marcy
- **NAVY –** George Bancroft
  John Young Mason (from September 9, 1846)
- **ATTORNEY GENERAL –** John Young Mason
  Nathan Clifford (from October 17, 1846)
  Isaac Toucey (from June 29, 1848)

The yellow area on this map indicates the part of Texas that sparked the Mexican War.

The Mexican War continued for the next two years. In 1848, the United States won. On February 2, both countries signed the Treaty of Guadalupe Hidalgo. This treaty ended the war.

Through the treaty, the United States acquired much land in the west. This land became known as the Mexican Cession. Today, it makes up California, Nevada, and Utah. It also includes parts of Arizona, New Mexico, Colorado, and Wyoming.

In addition, Mexico agreed to give up its claim to Texas. The boundary was set at the Rio Grande. The United States paid Mexico

$15 million for Texas and the Mexican Cession. Finally, Polk had achieved all of his goals as president.

The westward expansion of the country led to the creation of a new government agency. On March 3, 1849, Congress passed a bill to establish the Department of the Interior. It managed public parks, hospitals, and universities. The department also became responsible for exploring the new western U.S. lands.

At the end of his term, Polk refused to be renominated for president. He had worked hard and was tired. Polk was the first U.S. president to not seek reelection.

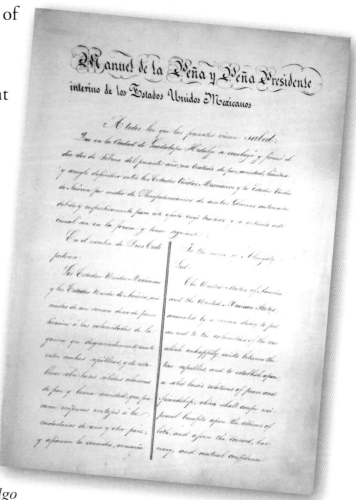

The Treaty of Guadalupe Hidalgo

HOME TO POLK PLACE

In 1849, Polk left the White House. He and his wife retired to Nashville, Tennessee. The journey was long, and Polk became sick. He relaxed for a few months in his home, Polk Place. But he never recovered.

On June 15, 1849, James K. Polk died. He was just 53 years old. Polk was buried in a Nashville cemetery. He was later reburied at Polk Place.

Mrs. Polk spent the rest of her life at Polk Place. She never remarried. In 1891, Sarah Polk died. She was buried beside her husband. In 1893, the Polks' remains were moved. Today, they are buried in a tomb on the grounds of the Tennessee Capitol in Nashville.

Polk was the first dark horse candidate to be nominated as U.S. president. Yet, he became an important political leader. While in office, he established an independent **treasury** and lowered **tariffs**.

Polk's tomb at the Tennessee Capitol

Polk also led the nation through the Mexican War. As a result, America reached from coast to coast. James K. Polk worked hard to be a strong leader for his country.

OFFICE OF THE PRESIDENT

BRANCHES OF GOVERNMENT

The U.S. government is divided into three branches. They are the executive, legislative, and judicial branches. This division is called a separation of powers. Each branch has some power over the others. This is called a system of checks and balances.

EXECUTIVE BRANCH

The executive branch enforces laws. It is made up of the president, the vice president, and the president's cabinet. The president represents the United States around the world. He or she oversees relations with other countries and signs treaties. The president signs bills into law and appoints officials and federal judges. He or she also leads the military and manages government workers.

LEGISLATIVE BRANCH

The legislative branch makes laws, maintains the military, and regulates trade. It also has the power to declare war. This branch consists of the Senate and the House of Representatives. Together, these two houses make up Congress. Each state has two senators. A state's population determines the number of representatives it has.

JUDICIAL BRANCH

The judicial branch interprets laws. It consists of district courts, courts of appeals, and the Supreme Court. District courts try cases. If a person disagrees with a trial's outcome, he or she may appeal. If the courts of appeals support the ruling, a person may appeal to the Supreme Court. The Supreme Court also makes sure that laws follow the U.S. Constitution.

QUALIFICATIONS FOR OFFICE

To be president, a person must meet three requirements. A candidate must be at least 35 years old and a natural-born U.S. citizen. He or she must also have lived in the United States for at least 14 years.

ELECTORAL COLLEGE

The U.S. presidential election is an indirect election. Voters from each state choose electors to represent them in the Electoral College. The number of electors from each state is based on population. Each elector has one electoral vote. Electors are pledged to cast their vote for the candidate who receives the highest number of popular votes in their state. A candidate must receive the majority of Electoral College votes to win.

TERM OF OFFICE

Each president may be elected to two four-year terms. Sometimes, a president may only be elected once. This happens if he or she served more than two years of the previous president's term.

The presidential election is held on the Tuesday after the first Monday in November. The president is sworn in on January 20 of the following year. At that time, he or she takes the oath of office:

I do solemnly swear (or affirm) that I will faithfully execute the office of President of the United States, and will to the best of my ability, preserve, protect and defend the Constitution of the United States.

LINE OF SUCCESSION

The Presidential Succession Act of 1947 defines who becomes president if the president cannot serve. The vice president is first in the line of succession. Next are the Speaker of the House and the President Pro Tempore of the Senate. If none of these individuals is able to serve, the office falls to the president's cabinet members. They would take office in the order in which each department was created:

Secretary of State

Secretary of the Treasury

Secretary of Defense

Attorney General

Secretary of the Interior

Secretary of Agriculture

Secretary of Commerce

Secretary of Labor

Secretary of Health and Human Services

Secretary of Housing and Urban Development

Secretary of Transportation

Secretary of Energy

Secretary of Education

Secretary of Veterans Affairs

Secretary of Homeland Security

Benefits

- While in office, the president receives a salary of $400,000 each year. He or she lives in the White House and has 24-hour Secret Service protection.

- The president may travel on a Boeing 747 jet called Air Force One. The airplane can accommodate 70 passengers. It has kitchens, a dining room, sleeping areas, and a conference room. It also has fully equipped offices with the latest communications systems. Air Force One can fly halfway around the world before needing to refuel. It can even refuel in flight!

- If the president wishes to travel by car, he or she uses Cadillac One. Cadillac One is a Cadillac Deville. It has been modified with heavy armor and communications systems. The president takes Cadillac One along when visiting other countries if secure transportation will be needed.

- The president also travels on a helicopter called Marine One. Like the presidential car, Marine One accompanies the president when traveling abroad if necessary.

- Sometimes, the president needs to get away and relax with family and friends. Camp David is the official presidential retreat. It is located in the cool, wooded mountains in Maryland. The U.S. Navy maintains the retreat, and the U.S. Marine Corps keeps it secure. The camp offers swimming, tennis, golf, and hiking.

- When the president leaves office, he or she receives Secret Service protection for ten more years. He or she also receives a yearly pension of $191,300 and funding for office space, supplies, and staff.

PRESIDENTS AND THEIR TERMS

PRESIDENT	PARTY	TOOK OFFICE	LEFT OFFICE	TERMS SERVED	VICE PRESIDENT
George Washington	None	April 30, 1789	March 4, 1797	Two	John Adams
John Adams	Federalist	March 4, 1797	March 4, 1801	One	Thomas Jefferson
Thomas Jefferson	Democratic-Republican	March 4, 1801	March 4, 1809	Two	Aaron Burr, George Clinton
James Madison	Democratic-Republican	March 4, 1809	March 4, 1817	Two	George Clinton, Elbridge Gerry
James Monroe	Democratic-Republican	March 4, 1817	March 4, 1825	Two	Daniel D. Tompkins
John Quincy Adams	Democratic-Republican	March 4, 1825	March 4, 1829	One	John C. Calhoun
Andrew Jackson	Democrat	March 4, 1829	March 4, 1837	Two	John C. Calhoun, Martin Van Buren
Martin Van Buren	Democrat	March 4, 1837	March 4, 1841	One	Richard M. Johnson
William H. Harrison	Whig	March 4, 1841	April 4, 1841	Died During First Term	John Tyler
John Tyler	Whig	April 6, 1841	March 4, 1845	Completed Harrison's Term	Office Vacant
James K. Polk	Democrat	March 4, 1845	March 4, 1849	One	George M. Dallas
Zachary Taylor	Whig	March 5, 1849	July 9, 1850	Died During First Term	Millard Fillmore

PRESIDENT	PARTY	TOOK OFFICE	LEFT OFFICE	TERMS SERVED	VICE PRESIDENT
Millard Fillmore	Whig	July 10, 1850	March 4, 1853	Completed Taylor's Term	Office Vacant
Franklin Pierce	Democrat	March 4, 1853	March 4, 1857	One	William R.D. King
James Buchanan	Democrat	March 4, 1857	March 4, 1861	One	John C. Breckinridge
Abraham Lincoln	Republican	March 4, 1861	April 15, 1865	Served One Term, Died During Second Term	Hannibal Hamlin, Andrew Johnson
Andrew Johnson	Democrat	April 15, 1865	March 4, 1869	Completed Lincoln's Second Term	Office Vacant
Ulysses S. Grant	Republican	March 4, 1869	March 4, 1877	Two	Schuyler Colfax, Henry Wilson
Rutherford B. Hayes	Republican	March 3, 1877	March 4, 1881	One	William A. Wheeler
James A. Garfield	Republican	March 4, 1881	September 19, 1881	Died During First Term	Chester Arthur
Chester Arthur	Republican	September 20, 1881	March 4, 1885	Completed Garfield's Term	Office Vacant
Grover Cleveland	Democrat	March 4, 1885	March 4, 1889	One	Thomas A. Hendricks
Benjamin Harrison	Republican	March 4, 1889	March 4, 1893	One	Levi P. Morton
Grover Cleveland	Democrat	March 4, 1893	March 4, 1897	One	Adlai E. Stevenson
William McKinley	Republican	March 4, 1897	September 14, 1901	Served One Term, Died During Second Term	Garret A. Hobart, Theodore Roosevelt

PRESIDENT	PARTY	TOOK OFFICE	LEFT OFFICE	TERMS SERVED	VICE PRESIDENT
Theodore Roosevelt	Republican	September 14, 1901	March 4, 1909	Completed McKinley's Second Term, Served One Term	Office Vacant, Charles Fairbanks
William Taft	Republican	March 4, 1909	March 4, 1913	One	James S. Sherman
Woodrow Wilson	Democrat	March 4, 1913	March 4, 1921	Two	Thomas R. Marshall
Warren G. Harding	Republican	March 4, 1921	August 2, 1923	Died During First Term	Calvin Coolidge
Calvin Coolidge	Republican	August 3, 1923	March 4, 1929	Completed Harding's Term, Served One Term	Office Vacant, Charles Dawes
Herbert Hoover	Republican	March 4, 1929	March 4, 1933	One	Charles Curtis
Franklin D. Roosevelt	Democrat	March 4, 1933	April 12, 1945	Served Three Terms, Died During Fourth Term	John Nance Garner, Henry A. Wallace, Harry S. Truman
Harry S. Truman	Democrat	April 12, 1945	January 20, 1953	Completed Roosevelt's Fourth Term, Served One Term	Office Vacant, Alben Barkley
Dwight D. Eisenhower	Republican	January 20, 1953	January 20, 1961	Two	Richard Nixon
John F. Kennedy	Democrat	January 20, 1961	November 22, 1963	Died During First Term	Lyndon B. Johnson
Lyndon B. Johnson	Democrat	November 22, 1963	January 20, 1969	Completed Kennedy's Term, Served One Term	Office Vacant, Hubert H. Humphrey
Richard Nixon	Republican	January 20, 1969	August 9, 1974	Completed First Term, Resigned During Second Term	Spiro T. Agnew, Gerald Ford

PRESIDENT	PARTY	TOOK OFFICE	LEFT OFFICE	TERMS SERVED	VICE PRESIDENT
Gerald Ford	Republican	August 9, 1974	January 20, 1977	Completed Nixon's Second Term	Nelson A. Rockefeller
Jimmy Carter	Democrat	January 20, 1977	January 20, 1981	One	Walter Mondale
Ronald Reagan	Republican	January 20, 1981	January 20, 1989	Two	George H.W. Bush
George H.W. Bush	Republican	January 20, 1989	January 20, 1993	One	Dan Quayle
Bill Clinton	Democrat	January 20, 1993	January 20, 2001	Two	Al Gore
George W. Bush	Republican	January 20, 2001	January 20, 2009	Two	Dick Cheney
Barack Obama	Democrat	January 20, 2009			Joe Biden

"No President who performs his duty faithfully and conscientiously can have any leisure." James K. Polk

WRITE TO THE PRESIDENT

You may write to the president at:

**The White House
1600 Pennsylvania Avenue NW
Washington, DC 20500**

You may e-mail the president at:
comments@whitehouse.gov

Glossary

annex - to take land and add it to a nation.

debate - a contest in which two sides argue for or against something.

Democrat - a member of the Democratic political party. When James K. Polk was president, Democrats supported farmers and landowners.

Democratic National Convention - a national meeting held every four years during which the Democratic Party chooses its candidates for president and vice president.

draft - to compose or prepare.

gallbladder - an internal organ that stores fluid from the liver.

gallstone - a mass of hardened minerals formed in the gallbladder.

inaugurate (ih-NAW-gyuh-rayt) - to swear into a political office.

parallel - an imaginary line around the earth that marks degrees of latitude.

running mate - a candidate running for a lower-rank position on an election ticket, especially the candidate for vice president.

secretary of state - a member of the president's cabinet who handles relations with other countries.

secretary of the treasury - a member of the president's cabinet that heads the U.S. Department of the Treasury. The secretary advises the president on financial policies and reports to Congress on the nation's finances. The secretary of the treasury is the U.S. government's chief financial officer.

slogan - a word or a phrase used to express a position, a stand, or a goal.

Speaker of the House - the highest-ranking member of the party with the majority in Congress.

Supreme Court - the highest, most powerful court of a nation or a state.

tariff - the taxes a government puts on imported or exported goods.

treasury - a place where money is kept.

tutor - to teach a student privately. The teacher is also called a tutor.

veto - the right of one member of a decision-making group to stop an action by the group. In the U.S. government, the president can veto bills passed by Congress. But Congress can override the president's veto if two-thirds of its members vote to do so.

Whig - a member of a political party that was very strong in the early 1800s but ended in the 1850s. Whigs supported laws that helped business.

WEB SITES

To learn more about James K. Polk, visit ABDO Publishing Company on the World Wide Web at **www.abdopublishing.com**. Web sites about James K. Polk are featured on our Book Links page. These links are routinely monitored and updated to provide the most current information available.

INDEX